WORKBOOK

MW01603202

WORKBOOK

(A GUIDE TO Mark Hyman's BOOK)

FOR

YOUNG FOREVER

The Secrets To Living Your Longest,

Healthiest Life.

Strategist Monroe

Disclaimer:

The information provided in this book is designed to provide helpful information on the subjects discussed.

WARNING: This book has passed cityscape and is free from plagiarism. False Copyright Claims will result in legal action taken.

Table of Contents

INTRODUCTION.

In "Young Forever," Mark Hyman explores the science of longevity and aging research, providing a roadmap for incorporating this knowledge into a self-care plan for living a healthy and long life. Before diving into the revolutionary science that can extend health span and life span, Hyman emphasizes the importance of determining one's "why" - the reason for wanting to live a longer and healthier life.

The book highlights the concept of ikigai, which the longest-lived people in the world, the Japanese, use to define their reason for being. Having purpose and meaning in life has been shown to promote longevity, regardless of lifestyle choices.

Hyman argues that the current perception of aging as inevitable decline and disease is flawed. He challenges the medical paradigm that focuses on downstream symptoms and diagnoses rather than addressing root causes and mechanisms of aging. Aging is not merely an inevitable consequence of time; it is a treatable condition.

The emerging field of functional medicine revolutionizes the understanding of health and disease by viewing the body as an interconnected ecosystem of networks and systems. Treating the underlying causes and hallmarks of aging can prevent, treat, and even reverse various chronic diseases.

The book is divided into three parts:

Part I: The Science of Longevity

•   The revolution in longevity science and the potential for reversing biological age.

•   The ten hallmarks of aging and how they relate to functional medicine.

Part II: The Why Behind the Young Forever Program

•   Optimizing core biological systems and understanding the science of eating and exercising for longevity.

•   Lifestyle practices for longevity, including hormesis and dealing with little stresses to activate longevity pathways.

•   Emerging advances in longevity treatments.

Part III: The How - The Young Forever Program

• Diagnosing and testing for underlying causes of aging.

• Using food, nutritional supplements, and lifestyle practices to activate longevity pathways.

• Personalizing the program to address individual needs and imbalances.

• Hyman shares his own longevity routine and commitment to living a long and healthy life.

The book ultimately encourages readers to redefine aging, embrace the science of healthy aging, and apply the principles and practices outlined in the Young Forever Program to experience profound changes in health and well-being. By living with purpose, maintaining optimal biological systems, and addressing the root causes of aging, individuals can live better, healthier, and more vibrant lives well beyond their golden years.

CHAPTER ONE.

THE QUEST FOR THE FOUNTAIN OF YOUTH: IS IMMORTALITY POSSIBLE?

The first chapter of Mark Hyman's book "Young Forever" explores the concept of aging, longevity, and the pursuit of immortality. The author questions whether disease and death are predetermined events that make us powerless victims or if the secrets to vitality and longevity are hidden within our DNA and biological networks.

The chapter delves into the historical examples of extraordinary longevity, such as Methuselah, Noah, and Adam from biblical times, as well as modern individuals like Madame Jeanne Calment and Emma Morano, who lived well beyond the average life expectancy. Additionally, the author introduces the concept of "Blue Zones," regions around the world where people live longer and healthier lives due to their unique lifestyles, nutrition, and community connections.

Hyman then shares his personal experiences visiting Sardinia's Blue Zone, where he witnesses the ancient ways of the Sardinians, their deep connection to nature, and their traditional food practices. He also explores the Blue Zone in Ikaria, Greece, where wild food and natural living contribute to longevity.

The chapter emphasizes the importance of adopting a functional medicine approach to aging, which focuses on identifying and addressing the root causes of diseases and aging. Hyman highlights the interconnectedness of the body's systems and how addressing imbalances can lead to increased health span and life span.

Workbook:

Discussion Questions:

1. What are your thoughts on the concept of living to 150 years old or beyond? Would you want to live that long? Why or why not?

----

2.   How do the Blue Zones provide insights into living longer and healthier lives? What specific lifestyle factors do you think contribute to their longevity?

----

3.   In what ways can you integrate the habits and behaviors of the Blue Zones into your own life to promote vitality and longevity?

----

4. How does the functional medicine approach differ from traditional medicine when it comes to addressing aging and disease? What do you think are the advantages of this approach?

Lessons:

1. Longevity and vitality are not predetermined; they can be influenced by lifestyle and environmental factors.

2.   The Blue Zones offer valuable lessons on living longer and healthier lives, emphasizing community, natural living, and nutrient-dense diets.

3.   Functional medicine provides a holistic approach to aging by addressing the root causes of diseases and imbalances in the body's systems.

4.   Advances in science and technology are opening up new possibilities for extending health span and life span.

Guides:

1.   Create your own "Blue Zone" within your community by fostering deep connections with family and friends and adopting healthy lifestyle practices.

2.   Embrace the principles of functional medicine by focusing on diet, exercise, stress management, and environmental factors that contribute to health and vitality.

3.   Stay informed about the latest advancements in longevity science and consider how they might impact your future health and aging.

4.   Develop a personalized plan for healthy aging by incorporating the lessons from the Blue Zones and functional medicine into your daily life.

Action Steps:

1.   Start incorporating more nutrient-dense foods into your diet, such as fresh fruits, vegetables, and whole grains.

2.   Engage in regular physical activity that you enjoy, whether it's walking, dancing, or practicing yoga.

3.   Prioritize social connections and spend time with loved ones regularly, fostering a sense of community and support.

4.   Reduce exposure to toxins and pollutants by choosing organic and natural products whenever possible.

Journal Prompts:

1.   Reflect on a time when you felt vibrant and healthy. What were the contributing factors to that feeling?

2.   Write about any fears or concerns you have regarding aging. How might you address these fears and create a more positive perspective on the aging process?

CHAPTER TWO
THE ROOT CAUSES OF AGING.

In this chapter the author delves into the root causes of aging and how they contribute to chronic diseases and a decline in overall health. Aging itself is seen as a disease, leading to various health issues and disabilities as people get older. The chapter emphasizes that most chronic diseases associated with aging, such as diabetes, cardiovascular disease, and dementia, share common underlying factors.

Hyman explains that while heart disease and cancer are significant contributors to mortality, eliminating these diseases would only increase the human lifespan by five to seven years. The real culprit behind chronic diseases and shortened lifespan is biological aging. As we age, our body's systems undergo various changes, leading to fatigue, decreased energy, diminished fitness levels, sleep problems, muscle loss, vision and hearing impairments, digestive issues, and memory decline.

The author highlights ten hallmarks of aging, including disrupted hormone and nutrient signaling, DNA damage, telomere shortening, damaged proteins, epigenetic damage, senescent cells, depleted energy, imbalances in gut health, stem cell exhaustion, and chronic inflammation. By understanding these hallmarks, it becomes possible to address the root causes of aging and the associated diseases.

The chapter introduces functional medicine, a paradigm that treats the whole body as an interconnected system, aiming to identify and correct underlying imbalances rather than merely managing symptoms. Functional medicine recognizes that many chronic diseases share common origins and advocates for lifestyle changes, such as a healthy diet, stress management, exercise, and adequate sleep, to optimize the body's natural healing and repair mechanisms.

Workbook:

Discussion Questions:

1.   How does the concept of aging as a disease challenge traditional views of getting older? How might this perspective impact the way we approach healthcare and wellness?

----

2.   The chapter suggests that most chronic diseases have common underlying factors. How can understanding these commonalities help us in preventing and managing chronic illnesses more effectively?

----

3. Functional medicine focuses on treating the root causes of health issues. What are some ways that conventional medicine might shift its approach to align with the principles of functional medicine?

----

4. The author mentions that many chronic diseases result from an imbalance in blood sugar and insulin resistance. How might dietary and lifestyle changes help prevent or reverse these conditions?

Lessons:

1.   Aging is a disease that affects every system in our body, leading to various chronic illnesses and a decline in overall health.

2.   Functional medicine treats the body as a whole system, aiming to identify and correct underlying imbalances that contribute to chronic diseases.

3.   The ten hallmarks of aging provide insights into the root causes of age-related diseases and offer potential targets for intervention and prevention.

4.   Lifestyle changes, such as a healthy diet, stress management, exercise, and proper sleep, can optimize the body's natural healing and repair mechanisms and promote longevity.

Action Steps:

1.   Conduct a Health Assessment: Schedule a health assessment with a qualified healthcare

practitioner to identify potential risk factors for chronic diseases and aging-related issues.

2.   Adopt a Plant-Rich Diet: Increase your intake of whole, plant-based foods, while reducing processed and sugary foods, to support overall health and longevity.

3.   Incorporate Exercise into Your Routine: Establish a regular exercise regimen that includes both cardiovascular activities and strength training to maintain muscle mass and overall fitness.

4.   Practice Stress Management: Develop stress-reduction techniques, such as meditation, mindfulness, or yoga, to support healthy aging and improve overall well-being.

Journal Prompts:

1.   Reflect on your current health status and identify any early signs of aging you may have experienced. How do these signs impact your daily life, and how do you feel about them?

2.   Consider the ten hallmarks of aging described in the chapter. Are there any specific hallmark(s) that you think might be affecting your health? How can you address these factors to improve your well-being?

CHAPTER THREE
BIOLOGICAL VERSUS CHRONOLOGICAL AGE.

In Chapter the author delves into the concept of biological age versus chronological age. He explains that while we cannot change our chronological age (determined by our birthdate), our biological age can accelerate or reverse based on the inputs to our biology. Recent scientific advancements allow us to measure biological age through the study of telomeres, which shorten as we age, and DNA methylation, a process that controls gene expression and interacts with our environment throughout life.

The epigenome, the software that runs our life program, is crucial in understanding healthy aging and longevity. While our genes are fixed, the genes expressed in our life's story can be modified through epigenetics. The exposome, comprising everything that has happened to us and our ancestors, plays a significant role in influencing our epigenome. From diet and exercise to stress and environmental exposures, every aspect of our life influences our biological age and health.

The chapter highlights several studies that demonstrate how lifestyle interventions and even certain medications can reverse biological age, making us biologically younger. Dr. Steve Horvath's study showed that a combination of human growth hormone, DHEA, and metformin reduced biological age by approximately two and a half years after a year of treatment. Other studies revealed the positive effects of vitamin D supplementation and adopting a Mediterranean diet in reversing biological age.

Workbook:

Discussion Questions:

1.　Do you believe that biological age is a better indicator of health and longevity than chronological age? Why or why not?

----

2.   How do you think DNA methylation and the exposome interact to determine our biological age?

----

3.   Based on the information provided, what lifestyle changes would you recommend to someone looking to reverse their biological age and improve their health?

----

4. In what ways do you think genetic testing and epigenetic analysis could be beneficial in personalized healthcare and disease prevention?

Lessons:

1. Biological age can be influenced and reversed through lifestyle interventions, providing opportunities for healthier and longer lives.

2. The epigenome plays a critical role in controlling gene expression and, thus, our health and aging process.

3.   Environmental factors and personal choices have a significant impact on biological age and overall well-being.

4.   Genetic testing and epigenetic analysis offer promising insights into personalized healthcare and disease prevention.

Action Steps:

1.   Schedule a Biological Age Test: Take proactive steps toward understanding your biological age by scheduling a telomere or DNA methylation test.

2.   Implement Epigenetic Health Strategies: Make changes to your lifestyle, such as adopting a nutrient-dense diet, practicing stress management techniques, and engaging in regular physical activity, to optimize your epigenome.

3.   Explore Longevity Interventions: Research and discuss with a healthcare professional potential longevity interventions that align with your health goals and values.

4.   Embrace Personalized Health: Consider exploring genetic testing and epigenetic analysis to gain personalized insights into your health and make informed decisions about your well-being.

Journal Prompts:

1. Reflect on Your Current Lifestyle: Take a moment to assess your current habits related to nutrition, exercise, stress management, sleep, and environmental exposures. How might they be influencing your biological age?

2. Epigenetic Influences: Think about specific life events, experiences, or exposures that may have had a lasting impact on your health and well-being. How do you think these epigenetic influences have shaped your biology?

3. Personal Health Goals: Write down your long-term health goals and aspirations. How do you envision your life in terms of health and vitality in the coming years?

4. Actionable Steps: Create a list of actionable steps you can take to improve your health and reverse your biological age. Consider both short-term and long-term changes you can make.

CHAPTER FOUR
THE HALLMARK OF AGING.

In this chapter, Mark Hyman delves into the ten hallmarks of aging, which are the underlying biological processes that contribute to the aging process. These hallmarks are interconnected and influenced by imbalances within the body. The author emphasizes the importance of understanding these hallmarks to develop strategies to slow down or even reverse aging.

Hallmark 1: Disrupted Hormone and Nutrient Signaling - Food and Aging: Hyman discusses how our modern diet and lifestyle interfere with the nutrient-sensing systems that regulate our biology. He highlights the importance of understanding how to eat to avoid disease and promote robust health, emphasizing the significance of a nutrient-rich diet to support longevity.

Hallmark 2: DNA Damage and Mutations - Problems with Our Genetic Blueprint: The author explains how DNA damage is a natural consequence of aging, occurring due to various factors like UV radiation, toxins, and stressors.

He discusses the role of sirtuins, which repair damaged DNA, and proposes lifestyle changes to minimize DNA damage and support repair mechanisms.

Hallmark 3: Telomere Shortening - Becoming Unraveled: Hyman delves into the concept of telomeres, protective caps at the ends of chromosomes that shorten with age. He discusses how telomere length impacts the aging process and suggests lifestyle practices, such as a phytonutrient-rich diet, exercise, and sleep, to lengthen telomeres.

Hallmark 4: Damaged Proteins - Malformed, Misshapen, Dysfunctional Molecules: The chapter explains how proteins regulate essential processes in the body and how their damage affects overall health. The author introduces autophagy, a recycling system that clears out damaged proteins, and advocates for lifestyle choices that promote this process.

Hallmark 5: Epigenetic Damage - A Dysfunctional Piano Player: Hyman explores epigenetics and how environmental factors influence gene expression. He emphasizes the impact of lifestyle choices on the epigenome and its role in either promoting health or contributing to disease.

Hallmark 6: Senescent Cells - The Attack of the Zombie Cells: The author describes senescent cells as damaged cells that don't die and cause inflammation and aging-related diseases. He highlights the importance of maintaining a healthy exposome to avoid the accumulation of senescent cells.

Hallmark 7: Depleted Energy - The Decline of Our Mitochondria: Hyman discusses mitochondria, the energy-producing organelles, and how their decline with age impacts energy levels and overall health. He outlines the factors that negatively affect mitochondria and offers strategies to support their function.

Hallmark 8: Of Microbes and Men - The Link Between Gut Health and Longevity: The chapter explores the gut microbiome's significance in overall health and longevity. Hyman emphasizes the role of a fiber-rich diet in fostering a healthy gut microbiome and its impact on immune functioning and chronic diseases.

Hallmark 9: Stem Cell Exhaustion - The Decline of Our Body's Rejuvenation System: The author explains how stem cells contribute to tissue repair and renewal and discusses the factors that age stem cells. He presents regenerative medicine options and lifestyle modifications that can maintain stem cell function.

Hallmark 10: Inflammaging - The Fire That Drives Chronic Disease and Shortens Life: Hyman delves into the relationship between aging and inflammation, emphasizing the importance of balancing inflammation through lifestyle modifications to prevent age-related chronic diseases.

Workbook:

Discussion Questions:

1.   What are some common dietary habits in modern society that contribute to disrupted hormone and nutrient signaling? How can we overcome these challenges and incorporate more nutrient-rich foods into our diets?

----

2.   How do you think understanding the role of epigenetic damage can empower individuals to make better lifestyle choices? What are some practical ways to positively influence our epigenome?

----

3.   Share your thoughts on the link between gut health and longevity. How might the depletion of gut microbes impact your overall health, and what steps can you take to improve your gut microbiome?

Lessons:

1.   Aging is a complex process influenced by various interconnected hallmarks within the body.

2.   A nutrient-rich diet, exercise, sleep, and stress management are key factors in maintaining a healthy aging process.

3.   Lifestyle choices, such as reducing sugar and processed food intake, can positively impact DNA, protein, and stem cell health.

4.   Understanding the importance of gut health and the microbiome can lead to improved overall health and longevity.

Guides:

1.   Guide to Nutrient-Rich Eating: Create a meal plan that includes a wide variety of fruits,

vegetables, whole grains, and healthy fats to support hormone and nutrient signaling.

2.   Autophagy Activation: Develop a fasting schedule or intermittent fasting plan to encourage the body's autophagy system to clear damaged proteins.

3.   Gut   Microbiome   Restoration: Incorporate high-fiber foods and probiotics into your diet to promote a healthy gut microbiome and reduce inflammation.

4.   Balancing   Inflammation: Identify sources of inflammation in your lifestyle and implement stress reduction techniques, exercise, and anti-inflammatory foods to maintain balanced inflammation levels.

Journal Prompts:

1.   Reflect on your current health status and any age-related concerns you may have. How do you feel about the aging process and your ability to influence it through lifestyle choices?

2.   Write about any changes you plan to make in your diet and lifestyle based on the information in this chapter. What challenges do you anticipate, and how will you overcome them?

CHAPTER FIVE

DYING OF TOO MUCH OR TOO LITTLE? WHY BALANCE MATTERS.

In this chapter the author discusses the intricate dance of chemical reactions happening within the human body and how imbalances can lead to aging and disease. Functional medicine, he explains, focuses on addressing the root causes of diseases and aging rather than just treating symptoms. The hallmarks of aging are primarily caused by imbalances – too much of harmful elements and too little of beneficial ones.

Hyman emphasizes that the exposome, which includes factors like diet, environmental toxins, infections, stress, and social isolation, plays a significant role in determining our health and aging risk. While genes are important, the exposome determines 90% of disease and aging risk. The author identifies various harmful elements that need to be reduced or eliminated to promote health, such as ultra-processed diets, environmental toxins, certain infections, gut-damaging medication, allergens, inactivity, and chronic stressors.

Conversely, he outlines the essential elements needed to restore balance and create health, including whole, real, unprocessed foods, regeneratively-raised meats, fiber, phytonutrients, micronutrients, optimal hormone levels, ideal light exposure, hydration, clean air, exercise, restorative practices, sleep, and community support.

Workbook

Discussion Questions:

1.   What are some of the key differences between conventional medicine and functional medicine in their approach to health and aging?

----

2.   How can our exposome significantly impact our disease and aging risk? How can we better manage our exposome to promote health?

----

3.   What are some of the harmful elements in modern diets, and how do they contribute to disease and aging? How can we improve our diet to support longevity?

----

4.   How does physical inactivity impact our health and contribute to the hallmarks of aging? What are some practical ways to incorporate more movement into daily life?

Lessons:

1.   Functional medicine focuses on addressing the root causes of diseases and aging by restoring balance to the body's ecosystem.

2.   The exposome, including diet, toxins, infections, and social factors, plays a significant role in determining health and aging risk.

3.   Harmful elements in diets, environmental toxins, inactivity, and chronic

stressors can lead to imbalances and accelerate aging.

4. Essential elements for health include whole, real foods, optimal nutrients, hormone balance, physical activity, sleep, and social connections.

Guides:

1. Guide to Identifying Imbalances: Learn to assess your lifestyle for potential imbalances and identify areas that need improvement to support health and longevity.

2. Guide to Optimizing Diet: Create a personalized plan to transition to a whole, nutrient-dense diet and reduce processed foods and harmful additives.

3. Guide to Integrating Exercise: Develop an exercise routine that suits your lifestyle and preferences, promoting regular movement and physical activity.

4. Guide to Building Community: Explore ways to strengthen your social connections, foster a sense of belonging, and cultivate meaningful relationships for improved well-being.

Action Steps:

1.   Perform a Lifestyle Audit: Assess your current diet, exercise routine, stress levels, and social connections to identify imbalances.

2.   Create a Balanced Meal Plan: Design a meal plan that emphasizes whole, unprocessed foods and includes essential nutrients for optimal health.

3.   Incorporate Daily Movement: Integrate at least 20 minutes of physical activity into your daily routine, such as walking, dancing, or yoga.

4.   Join a Community Group: Seek out local clubs, classes, or organizations that align with your interests to expand your social connections and support network.

Journal Prompts:

1.   How does the concept of functional medicine resonate with me, and how might it influence my approach to health and aging?

2.   What aspects of my exposome could be contributing to imbalances in my body, and how can I address them?

3.   Reflect on my current diet and lifestyle. What harmful elements could I reduce or eliminate, and what beneficial elements could I incorporate?

PART II: Optimizing Your Health Span and Life Span

CHAPTER SIX

FOUNDATION OF LONGEVITY: BALANCING YOUR SEVEN CORE BIOLOGICAL SYSTEM.

In this chapter, the focus is on the foundations of longevity and how to balance the seven core biological systems to achieve optimal health and longevity. These core systems include the microbiome, immune system, mitochondria, detoxification, circulation and transportation, communication, and structural system.

The chapter emphasizes the importance of the gut and the microbiome in maintaining overall health. A healthy gut with a balanced microbiome is crucial for nutrient absorption, immune function, and reducing inflammation. The author highlights the significance of a whole foods diet, high in prebiotic and probiotic foods, to maintain gut health.

The role of inflammation and its connection to chronic diseases and aging is explored in detail. The chapter emphasizes the importance of reducing chronic inflammation by avoiding toxins, stress, and a sedentary lifestyle while incorporating an anti-inflammatory diet and stress reduction techniques.

Mitochondria, the cellular powerhouses responsible for energy production, are discussed as key players in healthy aging. The chapter delves into various strategies such as calorie restriction, fasting, exercise, and specific phytochemicals to improve mitochondrial function and longevity.

Detoxification is also highlighted as a crucial process in maintaining health. The author stresses the importance of supporting and activating the body's detoxification systems to eliminate toxins and reduce the risk of chronic diseases.

The chapter explores the role of hormones, neurotransmitters, and cell-signaling molecules in maintaining a finely orchestrated communication system within the body. It discusses how hormone imbalances can accelerate aging and how hormonal optimization therapy, when necessary, can slow or prevent age-related changes.

Circulation and lymphatic flow are presented as essential for optimal health. The chapter emphasizes the importance of a healthy diet, exercise, and stress management to protect the cardiovascular system and improve lymphatic circulation.

The musculoskeletal system is discussed as a determinant of quality of life and longevity. The author stresses the significance of consuming high-quality proteins and essential nutrients for building and maintaining muscle and bone mass.

In summary, Chapter 6 lays the foundation for optimizing health span and life span by addressing the fundamental biological systems through diet, lifestyle, and targeted interventions.

Workbook:

Discussion Questions:

1.   How can we incorporate more prebiotic and probiotic foods into our daily diet to support a healthy gut and microbiome?

----

2.   In what ways can we reduce chronic inflammation in our daily lives, considering both dietary and lifestyle factors?

----

3.   What are some practical strategies for optimizing mitochondrial function and energy production in our bodies?

----

4.   How can we identify and reduce our exposure to environmental toxins to support our body's detoxification systems?

----

5.   What are some key lifestyle changes or interventions that can help balance hormones and promote healthy communication within our body?

Lessons:

1.   The gut and microbiome play a central role in overall health, and a whole foods diet high in prebiotic and probiotic foods is essential for gut health.

2.   Chronic inflammation is a significant driver of aging and chronic diseases, and reducing inflammation through diet and lifestyle can support healthy aging.

3.   Mitochondrial function is crucial for energy production and longevity, and various interventions like fasting and exercise can improve mitochondrial health.

4.   Detoxification is essential for eliminating toxins and promoting overall health, and supporting the body's detoxification systems through diet and lifestyle can have a profound impact on well-being.

Action Steps:

1.   Conduct a Gut Health Audit: Assess your current diet and identify opportunities to include more prebiotic and probiotic foods to support your gut health.

2.   Create an Anti-Inflammatory Meal Plan: Design a week-long meal plan that includes anti-inflammatory foods and avoids pro-inflammatory ingredients.

3.   Start a Mitochondrial-Boosting Exercise Routine: Incorporate regular exercise, such as high-intensity interval training or strength training, to support mitochondrial health.

4.   Implement Detoxification Strategies: Take steps to reduce your exposure to environmental toxins and support your body's detoxification pathways through diet and lifestyle changes.

Journal Prompts:

1.   Think about your current energy levels and any signs of fatigue. How might your mitochondrial health be affecting your energy production and overall vitality?

CHAPTER SEVEN
EATING FOR LONGEVITY

In this chapter, the focus is on optimizing health span and life span through proper nutrition. Hyman emphasizes that the foundational principles of staying healthy have remained constant throughout history and are crucial for reversing disease and extending both health span and life span. The new science of longevity provides insights into aging and how to biologically age more slowly. The core lifestyle factors for optimizing health span include nutrition, exercise, sleep, stress management, and relationships.

Hyman discusses the optimal longevity diet, which should consist of real, unprocessed foods that provide essential nutrients and phytonutrients. He highlights the importance of gut health and the microbiome, as it plays a vital role in regulating overall biological functions. To support the microbiome, he suggests consuming prebiotic and probiotic-rich foods.

The author emphasizes the role of food in immune system function and suggests avoiding inflammatory foods like sugar and refined oils. He recommends consuming antioxidant-rich foods to combat inflammation and support immunity. Hyman also delves into the significance of energy and mitochondria, advising the use of clean-burning fats and ketones for mitochondrial health.

Detoxification is another crucial aspect of longevity, and the chapter lists various foods that aid in detoxification, along with the detrimental effects of environmental toxins and medications.

Hyman discusses how nutrition affects communication and hormones within the body, especially in women, and the importance of balancing hormones and avoiding insulin resistance caused by excess sugar and starch consumption.

The chapter also highlights the importance of circulatory and lymphatic health and the role of nutrients in maintaining strong muscles, bones, and cells. Lastly, Hyman explores the concept of hormesis, where small amounts of stress from consuming phytochemicals in plant-based foods activate our innate healing systems.

Workbook

Discussion Questions:

1. What are some common dietary misconceptions that people tend to believe?

----

2. How can one strike a balance between plant-based and animal-based proteins to optimize protein intake?

----

3.   Discuss the role of stress and hormesis in promoting longevity and overall health.

----

4.   How can someone personalize their nutrition to address specific health concerns and goals?

Lessons:

1.   Prioritize nutrient-dense, real foods in your diet to support overall health and longevity.

2.   The gut and microbiome play a critical role in health, and it's essential to consume foods that support them.

3.   Proper detoxification is crucial for maintaining health and preventing chronic diseases.

4.   Balancing hormones and managing stress are key factors in promoting longevity and well-being.

Guides:

1.   A guide to creating a nutrient-dense meal plan tailored to your specific needs and health goals.

2.   A guide to incorporating prebiotic and probiotic foods into your diet to support gut health.

3.   A guide to reducing exposure to environmental toxins and adopting safer alternatives.

4.   A guide to practicing hormesis through various methods like intermittent fasting, exercise, and cold exposure.

Action Steps:

1.   Perform a thorough evaluation of your current diet and identify areas for improvement.

2.   Create a personalized meal plan focusing on nutrient-dense foods and gut-supportive elements.

3.   Implement a detoxification plan by reducing exposure to harmful substances and incorporating detoxifying foods.

4.   Begin an exercise regimen that includes strength training to support muscle and bone health.

Journal Prompts:

How do you plan to incorporate more prebiotic and probiotic foods into your diet, and what benefits do you expect to experience?

Write about your experience with stress management techniques and how they have influenced your health and longevity.

CHAPTER EIGHT
MOVING FOR LONGEVITY

In this chapter Hyman emphasizes the importance of regular exercise for optimizing health span and life span. The chapter starts with a quote highlighting that those who neglect physical activity will eventually have to face the consequences of illness. Hyman highlights the numerous benefits of exercise, which improve blood sugar control, insulin sensitivity, weight management, cardiovascular health, mood, cognitive function, bone health, muscle strength, and more. Additionally, exercise reduces the risk of various diseases, including certain cancers, and can even enhance sexual function.

The chapter explores the science behind exercise's positive effects on the body. Exercise activates various biological systems, including the microbiome, immune function, mitochondria, and hormonal balance. It triggers processes like autophagy, DNA repair, and the reduction of inflammation and oxidative stress, which all contribute to longevity and health.

Hyman stresses that exercise doesn't require excessive effort and can be as simple as walking for 10 minutes a day. However, he recommends incorporating more vigorous activity for 75 to 150 minutes a week, along with strength training exercises. He encourages readers to adopt a proactive approach to exercise to improve their health and extend their lives.

Workbook:

Discussion Questions:

1.   How does exercise impact the aging process and contribute to a longer, healthier life?

----

2.   What are some barriers you face when it comes to incorporating regular exercise into your life, and how can you overcome them?

----

3.   How can you motivate yourself and others around you to prioritize exercise and make it a consistent part of daily life?

----

4.   Discuss the link between exercise and other lifestyle factors like diet, sleep, and stress management. How do they interact to influence overall well-being?

Lessons:

1.   Regular exercise is a powerful tool for optimizing health and promoting longevity.

2.   Even simple activities like walking can have significant benefits for overall health.

3.   Exercise impacts various biological systems, contributing to improved immune function, hormone balance, and brain health.

4.   Combining strength training with aerobic exercises can lead to better muscle function and overall physical well-being.

Guides:

1.   Guide to Creating a Personalized Exercise Plan: Identify your fitness goals, preferences, and time constraints to design an exercise routine that suits your needs.

2.   Guide to Incorporating Movement Throughout Your Day: Find creative ways to stay active, such as taking short walks during breaks, using the stairs instead of elevators, or engaging in active hobbies.

3.   Guide to Overcoming Exercise Barriers: Address common obstacles to exercise, such as lack of time, motivation, or access to facilities, and develop strategies to overcome them.

4.   Guide to Progressive Exercise: Learn how to gradually increase the intensity and duration of your workouts to avoid injuries and maintain long-term motivation.

Action Steps:

1.   Assess your current fitness level and consult with a healthcare professional before starting any exercise program.

2.   Create a weekly exercise schedule that includes a mix of aerobic and strength training activities.

3.   Involve friends or family members in your exercise routine to increase accountability and make it more enjoyable.

4.   Track your progress and celebrate your achievements, no matter how small, to stay motivated and committed to your exercise goals.

Journal Prompts:

1.   How do you feel after engaging in physical activity? Describe the physical and emotional benefits you experience.

2.   Reflect on any positive changes you've noticed in your health and well-being since starting an exercise routine.

3.   Write about any challenges you face in maintaining a regular exercise habit and explore potential solutions.

4.   Imagine yourself living an active and healthy life in your later years. How does exercise contribute to that vision?

CHAPTER NINE

OPTIMIZING YOUR LIFESTYLE FOR

LONGEVITY: BEYOUND DIET AND EXERCISE.

In this chapter, Mark Hyman emphasizes that our daily behaviors and lifestyle choices are the most significant factors influencing our health and longevity. He highlights the importance of our individual exposome (the environmental factors that affect our genes) and how it determines our health rather than solely being determined by our genes.

The author draws inspiration from places like Sardinia and Ikaria, where many elderly residents have adopted daily habits that contribute to their vibrant and long lives. These habits include regular movement through gardening and hiking, managing stress, prioritizing sleep and naps, and having a deep sense of purpose and meaning.

Hyman suggests that after building a foundation of health-promoting habits, such as a proper diet and exercise routine, stress management, sleep, and fostering community and purpose, individuals can further enhance their longevity through practices like hormesis and advanced longevity innovations.

The chapter emphasizes the importance of nurturing the mind, heart, and spirit as crucial components of overall health. Neglecting mental and spiritual well-being can negatively impact physical health and even contribute to the development of diseases like cancer. Taking care of oneself, practicing self-compassion, cultivating a positive mind-set, building relationships, and finding a sense of purpose are essential for living a fulfilling and long life.

Hyman also underscores the significance of optimizing sleep for longevity. Sleep is crucial for overall health and affects various bodily systems, including the metabolism, mood, and cognitive function. Chronic sleep deprivation can lead to various health problems, including obesity, diabetes, heart disease, anxiety, depression, dementia, and an increased risk of certain cancers.

Finding meaning and purpose in life is another vital aspect of longevity. People who have a clear sense of purpose tend to live longer and have better overall well-being. The author suggests identifying one's passions, values, and gifts as a way to discover a sense of purpose.

In conclusion, Hyman emphasizes that incorporating health-promoting habits into daily life can significantly improve health and extend life span. For those seeking to explore more advanced strategies for longevity, the next chapters cover hormesis and regenerative medicine.

Workbook:

Discussion Questions:

1. How does the exposome affect our health, and what can we do to minimize its negative impact on our genes?

----

2. In what ways can stress management practices contribute to better health and longevity?

----

3. How does the concept of "self-care" align with the idea of prioritizing one's spirit and mental health?

----

4. Discuss the relationship between sleep and longevity. How can improving sleep habits lead to a longer and healthier life?

Lessons:

1.   Our daily behaviors and lifestyle choices have a profound impact on our health and longevity.

2.   Prioritizing mental and spiritual well-being is crucial for overall health and can positively influence physical health.

3.   Optimizing sleep is essential for longevity, as chronic sleep deprivation can lead to various health issues.

4.   Having a clear sense of purpose and meaning in life is associated with a longer and more fulfilling life.

.

Action Steps:

1.   Incorporate stress management techniques into your daily routine, such as meditation, deep breathing exercises, or spending time in nature.

2.   Create a sleep schedule and stick to it consistently, aiming for at least 7-9 hours of sleep each night.

3.   Engage in activities or practices that bring you joy and fulfillment, whether it's volunteering, pursuing a hobby, or spending time with loved ones.

4.   Prioritize self-care by setting aside time for relaxation, reflection, and mindfulness activities each day.

Journal Prompts:

1.   Reflect on a time when stress negatively impacted your health or well-being. What strategies could you have used to manage the stress better?

2.   Think about the things that bring you a sense of purpose and fulfillment. How can you incorporate more of these activities into your life?

3.   Write about an experience where practicing self-compassion led to positive changes in your behavior or well-being.

CHAPTER TEN
HOMEOSIS: ACTIVATING HEALING AND REPAIR MECHANISM

The chapter starts by highlighting the innate healing mechanisms present in the body that are designed to keep us healthy and alive. However, these mechanisms are often degraded by modern diet, environmental factors, and lifestyle choices. The key principle introduced is that moderate stress can make the body stronger and more resilient, akin to the effects of exercise.

The phenomenon of hormesis is explained as a process where small doses of adversity or abundance activate the body's self-protective mechanisms, leading to benefits such as DNA repair, reduced inflammation, increased antioxidant defenses, stem cell production, improved brain function, enhanced detoxification, and more. The chapter discusses various hormetic strategies for longevity, including time-restricted eating, fasting, high-intensity interval training, cold plunges, saunas, breath work, hypoxia, hyperbaric oxygen therapy, ozone therapy, light therapy, and the consumption of certain phytochemicals.

The concept of calorie restriction is explored as a potent hormetic strategy, although the challenge lies in finding ways to mimic its benefits without extreme dietary restrictions. Fasting, time-restricted eating, and ketogenic diets are mentioned as potential alternatives.

The chapter delves into the benefits of heat therapy, which involves exposing the body to high temperatures in saunas, steam baths, or hot yoga. Heat therapy activates heat shock proteins that aid in protein repair and play a role in reducing inflammation, improving cardiovascular fitness, and stimulating the release of growth hormone.

Conversely, cold therapy is discussed as another hormetic strategy, where brief exposures to cold temperatures, such as cold-water swimming or ice plunges, trigger beneficial physiological responses, including reduced inflammation and improved immune function.

The role of exercise in hormesis is emphasized, as all types of exercise stress the body in a positive way, leading to improved cardiovascular fitness, increased muscle mass, and enhanced overall health and longevity.

Light therapy is also explored, with a focus on the importance of managing light exposure to regulate circadian rhythms and maintain hormonal balance for optimal health.

The chapter further discusses the potential benefits of ozone therapy, which involves the therapeutic use of ozone to stimulate various health-promoting mechanisms in the body, such as reducing inflammation, enhancing immune function, and increasing stem cell production.

Lastly, the concept of hypoxia, or low-oxygen states, is explored as a hormetic stressor that activates various longevity pathways. It is observed in regions with high-altitude living and can be simulated using specific devices or breath work practices.

Workbook:

Discussion Questions:

1.   Which hormetic strategy from the chapter resonates with you the most, and why?

----

2.   How do you think hormetic strategies can be integrated into your daily routine or lifestyle?

----

3.   What are some challenges or obstacles you foresee in adopting hormetic practices, and how can you overcome them?

----

4.   Discuss how hormesis can be applied not only to physical health but also to mental and emotional well-being.

Lessons:

1. The body has innate healing mechanisms that can be activated through hormesis, providing numerous health benefits.

2. Moderate stressors, such as exercise, fasting, and temperature variations, can promote longevity and resilience in the body.

3. Hormetic strategies are diverse and can be tailored to individual preferences and lifestyles.

4. Consistency and gradual implementation of hormetic practices can lead to significant long-term health improvements.

Guides:

1. Guide to Implementing Time-Restricted Eating and Fasting for Hormetic Benefits

2. Guide to Incorporating Exercise and Strength Training into Your Daily Routine

3. Guide to Heat and Cold Therapy for Improved Health and Longevity

4. Guide to Light Therapy and Managing Light Exposure for Optimal Health

Action Steps:

1.　　Experiment with a time-restricted eating schedule, such as a 12- to 16-hour fasting window, and observe its impact on your energy levels and well-being.

2.　　Begin a regular exercise routine, incorporating both cardiovascular workouts and strength training, to experience the hormetic benefits of exercise.

3.　　Explore local facilities that offer sauna or steam therapy sessions, and aim to incorporate these into your weekly routine.

4.　　Investigate the use of light therapy devices, such as red-light therapy, and consider replacing LED or fluorescent bulbs with smart bulbs that adjust the light spectrum for the time of day.

Journal Prompts:

1.　　Reflect on your current health and well-being. How do you feel physically, mentally, and emotionally?

2.　　Consider specific health goals you would like to achieve, and identify hormetic strategies that align with these goals.

3.　　Write about any previous experiences with stress or adversity that have had positive impacts on your health or personal growth.

CHAPTER ELEVEN
ADVANCED LONGEVITY INNOVATIONS

In this chapter, the author explores the paradigm shift in medicine that views aging as a treatable disease rather than an inevitable part of getting older. He delves into advanced longevity innovations, including medical science, functional medicine, the microbiome, wearable and implantable bio trackers, quantum computing, machine learning, and artificial intelligence. These innovations are driving research and investments that promise to transform healthcare and longevity.

The chapter discusses cutting-edge therapies such as NAD+, rapamycin, stem cells, exosomes, peptides, natural killer cells, plasmapheresis, and ozone, which are already being used on the fringes of healthcare to optimize health and potentially extend life. The author also addresses the implications of achieving longevity escape velocity, where advances in medicine and technology could potentially outpace death. While the prospect of immortality raises complex societal, environmental, and ethical questions, the author emphasizes that advancements in extending health span can lead to significant economic and social benefits.

The future of healthcare and aging is expected to see remarkable changes, with the mapping of entire genomes, microbiomes, and metabolomes becoming routine, wearable and implantable devices tracking biomarkers in real-time, and artificial intelligence interpreting biological changes to optimize health proactively.

The chapter introduces promising therapies like regenerative medicine, which uses stem cells, exosomes, peptides, and placental matrix to rejuvenate tissues and support healing. The author shares personal experiences with these treatments and highlights their potential to treat chronic pain, injuries, and various health conditions effectively. The future may also witness the use of natural killer cells and therapeutic plasma exchange to address infections, cancer, and aging-related issues.

Workbook:

Discussion Questions:

1. Which advanced longevity innovation mentioned in the chapter excites you the most, and why?

----

2.   Do you believe that technologies like gene editing and nanobots, which are currently not available, have the potential to revolutionize healthcare and aging? Why or why not?

----

3. How do you think society should approach the possibility of living well beyond 100 years, and what challenges might arise in accommodating an aging population?

Lessons:

1. Aging can be viewed as a treatable disease, and advanced longevity innovations offer promising ways to optimize health and extend life.

2. Emerging therapies like stem cells, exosomes, peptides, and natural killer cells hold potential for regenerative medicine and promoting overall well-being.

3. The integration of wearable bio trackers, artificial intelligence, and genomic data will

revolutionize personalized healthcare and early disease detection.

4.   Achieving longevity escape velocity could have profound implications for society and the environment, necessitating thoughtful consideration and planning.

Action Steps:

1.   Research: Investigate further into advanced longevity innovations and the latest developments in regenerative medicine.

2.   Consultation: If interested, schedule a consultation with a qualified healthcare professional to explore potential therapies like stem cells or peptides.

3.   Lifestyle Optimization: Implement a healthful diet, exercise routine, and stress management practices to support longevity and overall well-being.

4.   Advocacy: Engage in discussions about the ethical, environmental, and societal implications of longevity escape velocity and advanced healthcare technologies.

PART III

THE YOUNG FOREVER PROGRAM

PART III: THE YOUNG FOREVER PROGRAM

CHAPTER TWELVE
THE YOUNG FOREVER PROGRAM OVERVIEW

In this chapter, the author discusses his desire to live a long and healthy life, aiming to reach the age of 120 or even 180. He believes this is possible for everyone by following the principles of the Young Forever Program. The program focuses on health span rather than just life span, emphasizing the importance of preventing chronic illness and reversing biological age.

The author acknowledges that longevity and aging research is rapidly advancing, but the foundational principles of preventing disease and promoting health are clear. Biological aging is seen as a treatable disease, and the hallmarks of aging are the key areas to target for treatment. The book addresses the root causes of aging and deterioration, which the author believes are not natural consequences of getting older but rather abnormalities caused by imbalances in the body's core biological systems.

The Young Forever Program is designed to address these imbalances through specific changes in diet and lifestyle, optimizing the body's systems. **The program includes:**

1. **Longevity Diet:** A diet rich in phytonutrients and mimicking calorie restriction.

2. **Optimizing Communication and Hormonal Balance:** Focusing on the body's hormonal systems.

3. **Boosting Energy Production and Eliminating Inflammation:** Improving energy levels and reducing inflammation.

4. **Restoring Gut Health:** Addressing gut imbalances and microbiome health.

5. **Reducing Toxic Exposures and Enhancing Detoxification:** Minimizing exposure to toxins and optimizing the body's detoxification processes.

6. **Strengthening Muscles, Bones, and Cells:** Improving physical health at the cellular level.

7. **Supporting Circulatory and Lymph Systems:** Maintaining healthy circulation and lymphatic function.

8.   **Balancing Mind, Heart, and Spirit:** Emphasizing mental and emotional well-being.

The Young Forever Program is built on sound scientific research, and the author believes that by addressing the root causes of aging and disease, it's possible to prevent or eliminate most age-related health conditions. The book also discusses emerging treatments for longevity, such as NAD+ and stem cell therapy, which are becoming more accessible.

The chapter concludes with a guide on how to use the Young Forever Program, starting with identifying core physiological imbalances through quizzes and functional medicine testing. The program gradually incorporates changes in diet, supplements, lifestyle practices, and advanced longevity strategies. The author emphasizes that each person's approach to the program can be tailored based on their preferences and comfort levels.

Workbook:

Discussion Questions:

1.   Do you believe that living to 120 or beyond in good health is achievable? Why or why not?

----

2. What aspects of the Young Forever Program resonate with you the most, and which ones do you find challenging?

----

3. How do you think advances in longevity research will impact healthcare and society in the future?

----

4.   What are some barriers you may face in implementing the Young Forever Program, and how can you overcome them?

Lessons:

1.   The Young Forever Program emphasizes health span over life span, focusing on preventive measures to maintain good health as you age.

2. Biological aging is treatable, and by addressing imbalances in core biological systems, it's possible to reverse the hallmarks of aging.

3. A longevity diet rich in phytonutrients, coupled with targeted supplements and hormetic therapies, can support age-reversing processes.

4. Advances in longevity research may soon make age-reversal treatments more accessible and commonplace.

Guides:

1. Young Forever Quizzes: Identify your core physiological imbalances and assess areas for improvement.

2. Young Forever Function Health Panel: Get a baseline panel of longevity laboratory testing for better health insights.

3. Longevity Diet: Follow the Young Forever Program's dietary recommendations to promote health and longevity.

4. Young Forever Lifestyle Practices: Incorporate exercise, sleep optimization, stress management, and mindfulness into your daily routine.

Action Steps:

1. Complete the Young Forever Quizzes to assess your core physiological imbalances.

2. Consider getting a baseline panel of longevity laboratory testing to better understand your health status.

3. Adopt the Young Forever Longevity Diet and explore adding the Young Forever Supplements for Longevity.

4. Implement the Young Forever Lifestyle Practices, including exercise, sleep optimization, and stress reduction techniques.

Journal Prompts:

1. Reflect on your long-term health goals. How does the Young Forever Program align with these aspirations?

3. Identify one core biological system that you would like to optimize. What steps can you take to achieve this goal?

4. Imagine your life at 120 years old, living in good health. What would you like your daily routine to look like at that age? How can you start incorporating some of those elements into your life now?

CHAPTER THIRTEEN
THE YOUNG FOREVER PROGRAM: TESTING

In this chapter Mark Hyman, the author discusses the importance of diagnostic testing in promoting health and longevity. He highlights the limitations of traditional medical tests that often focus on surrogate markers and suggests functional medicine as a more comprehensive approach. The chapter covers various types of testing, including genetic testing, quantified-self metrics with wearable devices, and functional medicine testing for core biological systems. Additionally, the chapter includes quizzes to assess the readers' health in different areas and encourages personalized self-care based on the results.

Engaging Question:

How do you think the integration of wearable devices and quantified-self metrics in healthcare will impact the future of medical treatments and prevention strategies?

Lesson:

Traditional medical testing often focuses on surrogate markers, but functional medicine testing provides a more comprehensive view of our biological systems, enabling personalized self-care.

Guide:

The chapter offers guidance on different types of testing, including genetic testing, quantified-self metrics using wearable devices, and functional medicine testing for various core biological systems.

Action Steps:

1. Research and consider getting genetic testing to understand your unique gene variations and potential health risks.

2. Explore wearable devices and incorporate quantified-self metrics to track

important health indicators like heart rate, sleep, and exercise.

3. Assess your core biological systems using the provided quizzes and consider seeking further testing if severe imbalances are detected.

4. Consult a functional medicine practitioner for a more comprehensive health assessment and personalized health plan.

Journal Prompt: Reflect on your current approach to healthcare and testing. What aspects of functional medicine and personalized testing appeal to you the most, and how do you envision implementing these practices into your self-care routine?

CHAPTER FOURTEEN
THE YOUNG FOREVER LONGEVITY DIET: FOOD AS MEDICINE

This chapter introduces "The Young Forever Longevity Diet: Food as Medicine." The chapter emphasizes the importance of using food to promote health and longevity, acknowledging the need for personalized nutritional recommendations based on individual biology. It presents the Pegan Diet as a flexible framework that combines the principles of quality, food as medicine, and personalization.

The Pegan Diet encourages a focus on plant-based foods, with about three-quarters of the plate consisting of veggies, particularly non-starchy varieties. Low-glycemic fruits like berries and kiwis are recommended, while high-glycemic fruits should be consumed occasionally. Healthy fats from sources such as nuts, seeds, olive oil, avocados, and small wild fatty fish are essential components of the diet. Animal products should be consumed in moderation, with an emphasis on regeneratively raised, grass-fed, or organic options.

The chapter advises avoiding or limiting sugar, grain, bean, and seed oils, as well as conventional dairy, and instead suggests considering alternatives like goat or sheep products and nut milks. Foods contaminated with pesticides, herbicides, antibiotics, and hormones should also be reduced or avoided, and GMO foods should be minimized or excluded. The focus is on eating nutrient-dense, nourishing foods that promote vitality and well-being.

In addition to the dietary recommendations, the chapter highlights the concept of "Pegan Fats," identifying individuals who may experience adverse reactions to saturated fats. The Longevity Superfoods section introduces phytochemicals as powerful compounds found in various foods that can potentially support longevity. The chapter concludes by discussing strategies to mimic calorie restriction, such as time-restricted eating, intermittent fasting, fasting-mimicking diets, and the ketogenic diet, which may activate longevity pathways.

Workbook:
Discussion Questions:

1. What are the key principles of the Pegan Diet, and how do they contribute to overall health and longevity?

----

2. How can individuals determine if they are lean mass hyper-responders (LMHRs) and how might this affect their dietary choices?

----

3. What are some of the longevity superfoods mentioned in the chapter, and how can you incorporate them into your daily diet?

----

4. Discuss the various strategies to mimic calorie restriction. Which one do you find most feasible and appealing, and why?

Lessons:

1.   Food is a powerful tool for promoting health and longevity, and adopting a nutrient-dense, plant-based diet can have significant benefits.

2.   Personalizing your diet to suit your own biology and preferences is essential for achieving optimal results and sustainable dietary habits.

3.   Lean mass hyper-responders may need to adjust their fat intake, and listening to your body's response to different fats can guide dietary choices.

4.   Phytochemicals found in various foods can play a crucial role in supporting longevity, and incorporating these foods into your diet can be beneficial.

Guides:

1.   "Pegan Fats" List: Identify fats that may be better suited for individuals who are lean mass hyper-responders.

2.   Longevity Superfoods: A list of phytochemical-rich foods that support vitality and well-being.

3. Calorie Restriction Mimicking Strategies: An overview of different approaches to mimic calorie restriction and promote longevity.

4. Regenerative and Sustainable Food Choices: Tips for choosing foods that are good for both human health and the environment.

Action Steps:

1. Assess your current diet and make adjustments to align with the Young Forever Longevity Diet principles.

2. Experiment with time-restricted eating or intermittent fasting to explore their potential benefits for your health and well-being.

3. Incorporate longevity superfoods into your meals regularly to provide your body with essential phytochemicals.

4. Explore sustainable and regeneratively raised food options to support both personal health and the health of the planet.

Journal Prompts:

1. How does your current diet make you feel? What changes could you make to improve your overall well-being?

CHAPTER FIFETEEN
THE YOUNG FOREVER SUPPLEMENT FOR
LONGEVITY

In this chapter the author discusses the importance of nutritional and herbal supplements for promoting longevity. He acknowledges that the topic of supplements can be confusing due to misinformation and lack of regulation in the industry. However, he argues that the role of nutrients in our body's biochemical processes is crucial, and deficiencies can lead to various health issues, including chronic diseases and accelerated aging.

Hyman emphasizes that most people are deficient in one or more nutrients, even if they believe they have a balanced diet. He recommends that everyone should consider taking foundational supplements such as a good multivitamin and mineral, vitamin D3, omega-3 fats, magnesium, and probiotics. These supplements serve as essential insurance against the nutrient-depleted modern diet, toxic environment, and high-stress lifestyles that many people experience.

The author divides supplements into two categories: foundational nutrients for everyone and specifically targeted supplements based on individual needs such as genetics, age, lifestyle, and health conditions. He provides a core plan of recommended supplements, including vitamin D3, EPA/DHA (omega-3), multivitamins, additional methylation support, and magnesium. For those interested in further optimizing longevity, he introduces the advanced longevity support supplements, which target specific pathways associated with aging and longevity.

The advanced longevity stack includes compounds like NMN or NR (NAD+ precursors), fisetin (a potent senolytic), quercetin, pterostilbene, curcumin, EGCG (from green tea), glucoraphanin (from broccoli-seed extract), urolithin A, and sarcopenia support supplements like branched-chain amino acids and creatine.

The author also mentions that the field of longevity medications is rapidly evolving, and certain drugs like metformin and rapamycin are being studied for their potential to optimize health and aging. However, he advises caution in using these medications until more research is available or after consulting with a healthcare professional.

Workbook:

Discussion Questions:

1. Why is the lack of regulation in the supplement industry a cause for concern?

----

2. What are some potential benefits and risks associated with taking advanced longevity support supplements?

----

3.   How does the modern lifestyle contribute to nutrient deficiencies?

----

4.   Do you think it's necessary for everyone to take foundational supplements, or should it be based on individual circumstances?

Lessons:

1.   Understanding the role of nutrients in our body's biochemical processes is essential for maintaining optimal health and longevity.

2.   Nutritional deficiencies are widespread in the modern population, even in those who believe they have a balanced diet.

3.   Foundational supplements can serve as insurance against the nutrient-depleted modern diet, toxic environment, and high-stress lifestyles.

4.   Advanced longevity support supplements target specific pathways associated with aging and longevity and may provide additional health benefits.

Action Steps:

1.   Evaluate Your Nutritional Status: Consider getting your nutritional levels tested to identify potential deficiencies.

2.   Review Your Supplement Plan: Assess your current supplement intake and determine

if adjustments are needed based on your unique needs.

3. Research Reputable Brands: Explore reliable supplement brands that adhere to good manufacturing practices and undergo third-party testing.

4. Consult with a Healthcare Professional: Discuss your supplement plan with a qualified healthcare practitioner to ensure it aligns with your health goals and conditions.

Journal Prompts:

1. Reflect on Your Supplement Journey: Describe your experiences with supplements, including any noticeable effects or changes in your health.

2. Personalizing Your Longevity Plan: Consider your genetics, lifestyle, and health conditions to identify specific supplements that may benefit you.

3. Exploring Longevity Medications: Express your thoughts and concerns about potential longevity medications like metformin and rapamycin.

CHAPTER SIXTEEN
THE YOUNG FOREVER LIFESTYLE PRACTICE: HOW TO EXERCISE, DE-STRESS, SLEEP, FIND YOUR PURPOSE AND ACTIVATE HORMESIS.

This chapter discusses The Young Forever Lifestyle Practices, focusing on exercise, stress reduction, sleep optimization, finding purpose, and activating hormesis. The chapter emphasizes the importance of these practices for enhancing health, longevity, and overall well-being.

1. **Exercise:** The chapter emphasizes the significance of regular exercise for health and longevity. Aerobic conditioning, strength training, and flexibility are essential components of a well-rounded exercise routine. High-intensity interval training (HIIT) is highlighted as a potent method for boosting metabolism, losing weight, and increasing VO2 max.

2. **Stress Reduction:** The chapter explores various techniques to manage and reduce stress, acknowledging the impact of chronic stress on overall health. Breathing practices, meditation, yoga, and journaling are

recommended to help cope with stress effectively.

3. **Sleep Optimization:** Optimal sleep is critical for longevity. The chapter provides practical tips for improving sleep quality, such as maintaining a regular sleep schedule, creating a calming sleep environment, and avoiding caffeine and electronics before bedtime.

4. **Finding Purpose:** The chapter discusses the significance of having a sense of purpose and meaning in life. Tips for discovering one's purpose and connecting with a community are provided.

5. **Activating Hormesis:** The chapter introduces hormesis as a process of safely stressing the body to stimulate resilience and longevity. Calorie restriction, hot and cold therapy, phytohormesis through consuming phytochemical-rich foods, and advanced hormesis therapies like hyperbaric oxygen therapy and ozone therapy are discussed.

Workbook:

Discussion Questions:

1.   Which exercise routine do you enjoy the most, and how can you incorporate it into your daily life?

----

2.   How do you currently manage stress, and what additional stress reduction techniques could you try?

----

3.   What changes can you make in your sleep habits to optimize your sleep and improve your overall health?

----

4.   Have you ever tried any hormesis practices? If not, which ones are you interested in exploring, and why?

Lessons:

1.   Regular exercise, stress reduction, and optimal sleep are essential for a long and healthy life.

2.   Finding meaning and purpose in life can enhance well-being and increase longevity.

3.   Hormesis practices, such as calorie restriction and hot/cold therapy, can stimulate resilience and promote longevity.

4.   Engaging in a growth mindset, serving others, and cultivating passions contribute to a fulfilling and purposeful life.

Guides:

1.   Exercise Guide: Develop a personalized exercise routine that includes aerobic conditioning, strength training, and flexibility exercises.

2.   Stress Reduction Guide: Create a stress reduction plan that includes breathing practices, meditation, journaling, and yoga.

3.   Sleep Optimization Guide: Establish a sleep schedule, create a calming sleep environment, and implement strategies to promote restful sleep.

4.   Hormesis Activation Guide: Experiment with hormesis practices like intermittent

fasting, cold showers, and consuming phytochemical-rich foods.

Action Steps:

1. Schedule regular exercise sessions based on your fitness goals and preferences.

2. Incorporate stress reduction techniques into your daily routine, such as deep breathing exercises and meditation.

3. Create a sleep-friendly environment in your bedroom, and develop a bedtime routine to promote better sleep.

4. Introduce hormesis practices into your life gradually, starting with intermittent fasting or cold showers.

Journal Prompts:

1. Reflect on your exercise habits: What type of exercise do you enjoy the most, and how can you make it a regular part of your life?

2. Write about your stress management techniques: Which techniques have been most effective in reducing your stress levels?

3. Consider hormesis practices: Are you open to trying hormesis techniques, and if so, which ones are you most interested in exploring?

CHAPTER SEVENTEEN
THE YOUNG FOREVER PLAN TO OPTIMIZE YOUR SEVEN CORE BIOLOGICAL SYSTEM.

In this chapter, the focus is on the Young Forever Program, which aims to correct imbalances in the seven core biological systems. The author emphasizes that personalized health and longevity plans can be developed by following specific steps:

1.   **Identify imbalances:** Take quizzes in Chapter 13 to determine which core biological systems are out of balance. Scores between 10 and 50 percent indicate a need for focused recommendations, while scores over 50 percent may require additional help from a functional medicine doctor.

2.   **Establish a baseline:** Get the Young Forever Function Health Panel to map out testing and consider additional tests from Chapter 13 if imbalances persist.

3.   **Implement healing strategies:** Address imbalances in core systems, starting with the gut (Core System 1) and the immune system (Core System 2), as these often correct imbalances in other systems.

4.   **Seek professional help if needed:** If symptoms persist or scores do not improve, consult a functional medicine practitioner.

The following sections provide a detailed summary of the recommendations for each core system:

Core System 1: Microbiome and Gut Optimization

•   Remove potential allergens and inflammatory foods through an elimination diet.

•   Avoid gut-busting drugs like NSAIDs, antibiotics, steroids, and acid blockers.

•   Test for and treat parasites and bad bacteria and yeast overgrowth.

•   Replenish digestive enzymes, take prebiotic supplements, and support the microbiome with probiotics.

•   Increase intake of polyphenols and consider using bovine immunoglobulins for gut healing.

•   Explore fecal matter transplants (FMT) for treating diseases and supporting gut health.

Core System 2: Immune and Inflammatory Optimization

• Follow an anti-inflammatory elimination diet to reduce inflammation.

• Treat infections and address mold toxicity.

• Use senolytics to target and kill zombie cells that cause inflammation.

• Explore peptides and therapies like ozone, hyperbaric oxygen, and hyperthermia for immune support.

Core System 3: Mitochondria and Energy Optimization

• Adopt the Young Forever Longevity Diet, low in starch and sugar, high in good fats and phytochemicals.

• Eliminate or reduce environmental toxins.

• Practice hormesis with various techniques like intermittent fasting and cold and hot therapies.

• Take the Young Forever Supplements and consider additional mitochondria therapies.

• Use red-light therapy to boost energy production in mitochondria.

Core System 4: Detoxification Optimization

• Reduce toxic exposures and enhance body's detoxification systems.

• Upregulate detoxification pathways with detoxifying foods and supplements.

• Treat heavy metal burden and address mold toxicity.

Core System 5: Optimizing Communication, Hormone Balance, and Metabolic Health

• Consume a low-refined-carbohydrate, higher-fat, high-fiber, phytonutrient-rich diet.

• Exercise, take Core Supplement Plan, and consider additional supplements for glucose and insulin optimization.

Core System 6: Transport Optimization

• Eat the Young Forever Longevity Diet and move regularly to support circulatory and lymphatic systems.

• Try yoga, sauna therapy, and massage to promote circulation and lymph flow.

Core System 7: Structural Optimization

• Engage in regular exercise, strength training, and flexibility programs.

• Use supplements, peptide therapy, and prolozone therapy to reduce pain and repair tissues and joints.

Optimizing Nutritional Status

• Take the Core Supplement Plan and add specialized forms of B vitamins if needed.

Optimizing Mind-Body-Spirit Healing

• Seek support through therapy, dynamic neural retraining, ketamine therapy, and stellate ganglion block for emotional healing.

• Explore emerging psychedelic treatments for mental, emotional, and spiritual health.

Workbook:

Discussion Questions:

1. How does the Young Forever Program differ from conventional approaches to health and longevity?

----

2.   Have you ever considered personalized health plans or functional medicine practices? Why or why not?

----

3.   Which core biological system do you think needs the most attention in your life, and how do you plan to address it?

----

4.   Are there any specific diet, lifestyle, or supplement recommendations from the book that you find challenging to implement? How can you overcome these challenges?

----

5.   What are your thoughts on the potential of emerging therapies like peptide therapy and psychedelic treatments for mental and emotional healing?

Lessons:

1.   The Young Forever Program emphasizes personalized health plans based on individual imbalances in the seven core biological systems.

2.   Healing the gut is essential for healthy aging and longevity, and specific steps like an elimination diet and probiotic support can aid in gut optimization.

3.   Chronic inflammation plays a significant role in aging and can be addressed through an anti-inflammatory elimination diet and targeted therapies like ozone therapy and peptides.

4.   Supporting mitochondria and energy optimization involves adopting a low-refined-carbohydrate diet, engaging in hormesis, and

considering additional supplements for mitochondrial health.

Action Steps:

1.   Take the quizzes in Chapter 13 to assess the imbalances in your core biological systems.

2.   Get the Young Forever Function Health Panel to establish a baseline for testing.

3.   Implement diet, lifestyle, and supplement recommendations for healing the identified imbalances.

4.   Engage in hormesis practices, such as intermittent fasting and cold therapies, to support mitochondria and energy optimization.

Journal Prompts:

1.   Describe your current health and any symptoms or imbalances you experience.

2.   Reflect on your dietary choices and identify potential allergens or inflammatory foods that you consume regularly.

3.   Write about your experience with any past therapies or treatments for chronic inflammation, if applicable.

CHAPTER EIGHTEEN
DR HYMAN'S YOUNG FOREVER PROGRAM: PUTTING IT ALL TOGETHER.

In this chapter Mark Hyman shares the Young Forever Program, which has helped him maintain strength, health, and youthfulness even at the age of sixty-three. The program is designed to slow or reverse aging and improve overall well-being. Dr. Hyman emphasizes the importance of choosing practices that resonate with each individual and can be incorporated into their daily lives.

The Young Forever Program consists of several key components:

1. Diet: Dr. Hyman follows the Pegan Diet, which emphasizes high levels of phytochemicals known to support longevity pathways and combat aging. He includes a daily Healthy Aging Shake to build muscle.

2. Exercise: Dr. Hyman engages in four to six days of aerobic exercise with interval training, including biking, tennis, hiking, and swimming. He also incorporates strength training using resistance bands and practices yoga regularly.

3. Sleep: Dr. Hyman prioritizes 7 to 8 hours of sleep each night, using magnesium glycinate and creating a restful sleep environment with eyeshades and earplugs. He tracks his sleep and biomarkers with devices like the Oura Ring and Eight Sleep system.

4. Stress Management: Dr. Hyman practices mantra meditation and breath work daily to manage stress. He spends time in nature, engages in play and adventures with friends and family, and receives regular massages.

5. Hormesis: Dr. Hyman adopts time-restricted eating and incorporates potent phytohormesis plant compounds in his diet. He uses saunas, cold plunges, red-light therapy, and other therapies to promote hormesis and stimulate adaptive responses in the body.

6. Basic Supplement Plan: Dr. Hyman takes various supplements to support his overall health, including vitamins, omega-3 fatty acids, and specific compounds known for their longevity-promoting effects.

7. Advanced Longevity Therapies: As a longevity pioneer, Dr. Hyman has explored emerging therapies, such as peptide therapy, stem cells, exosomes, and more, to address chronic injuries and improve overall health. These therapies require further research but have shown promise in enhancing well-being.

8. Meaning, Purpose, and Mental Health: Dr. Hyman finds fulfillment in meaningful work that serves others and engages in exploring spiritual traditions. He emphasizes the importance of mental health and mindset, seeking support from a life coach and friends.

9. Community and Connection: Dr. Hyman cultivates a supportive community of friends and colleagues, participating in a weekly support group to foster personal and professional growth.

Workbook:

Discussion Questions:

1. What aspects of Dr. Hyman's Young Forever Program do you find most intriguing or inspiring?

2.　How do you think the Young Forever Program can be adapted to fit different individual needs and lifestyles?

3.　Are there any components of the program that you are already practicing in your life? How have they benefited you?

----

4.   Dr. Hyman mentions exploring advanced longevity therapies. What are your thoughts on these emerging therapies, and would you be open to trying them in the future?

Lessons:

1.   Longevity and youthful vitality can be achieved through a holistic approach that includes diet, exercise, sleep, stress management, and meaningful connections.

2.   Customization   and   gradual incorporation of lifestyle practices are key to long-term success in improving health and well-being.

3.   Embracing emerging therapies with caution and informed awareness can offer potential benefits for overall health.

4.   Prioritizing mental health and seeking support from others can positively impact well-being and life satisfaction.

Action Steps:

1.   Evaluate Your Diet: Assess your current diet and identify areas where you can include more phytochemical-rich foods. Consider incorporating Dr. Hyman's Healthy Aging Shake into your routine.

2.   Engage in Regular Exercise: Commit to a regular exercise routine that includes both aerobic activities and strength training, along with yoga or stretching sessions.

3.   Prioritize Sleep: Aim for 7 to 8 hours of quality sleep each night, and create a relaxing sleep environment with the use of sleep aids like magnesium glycinate, eyeshades, and earplugs.

4. Explore Stress-Relief Techniques: Experiment with different stress management practices, such as meditation, breath work, or spending time in nature, to find what works best for you.

Journal Prompts:

1. How do you envision your ideal version of a "Young Forever" lifestyle? Describe the activities, habits, and practices that would make up your personalized program.

2. Reflect on your current state of health and well-being. What aspects do you feel are lacking, and how can you incorporate elements of the Young Forever Program to address those areas?

3. Write about any experiences you've had with hormesis or advanced longevity therapies. Are you open to exploring these in the future?

Made in United States
North Haven, CT
02 February 2025

65295131R00068